Su-27 FLANKER
SUKHOI SUPERFIGHTER

Su-27 FLANKER
SUKHOI SUPERFIGHTER

JON LAKE

OSPREY
AEROSPACE

Acknowledgements

I owe a debt of gratitude to many friends who have given pictures, help and encouragement. I am especially grateful to my partner in crime and co-editor of 'World Air Power Journal', David K Donald, and to Martin Baumann, John W R Taylor OBE, Bill Green, Bill Gunston, Grant 'Secret Policeman's Land Rover' Race, Peter J Cooper and son Richard (who will do us all out of our jobs in a few years!), Nigel Eastaway, Robert J Ruffle, Paul Bennett and Simon Watson, and to Joe Cupido, Arnold Swanberg, Jeff Wilson, Peter Wilson, Peter West, Robert F Dorr, and Peter Mersky in the United States. Thanks too go to those at Sukhoi, who patiently answered my many questions, especially Yevgeni Frolov, Victor Pugachev, and Mikhail Simonov. Penultimately, my thanks go to Osprey Aerospace editors Dennis ('The Menace') Baldry (but don't ask him about his personal method of wine-tasting), and the irrepressible Tony Holmes. Lastly, thank you Jilly, for your encouragement, patience and tolerance, and during the long and tortuous course of this book, becoming my wife.

Front cover Maintaining a loose deuce formation over the lush Russian countryside, a pristine pair of Su-27s from a fully operational frontline unit (*Via Carey Schofield*)

Back cover *Flankers* on the flightline of an unidentified IA-PVO base. 'Red 32' in the background is 'cranked up' and ready to go, but the pilot in the foreground, forlornly sitting on a tow bar, is clearly unhappy about the serviceability of his aircraft! (*Via Carey Schofield*)

Title page Climb aboard for the flight of your life. Clearly marked with its Sukhoi display number, Su-27 'Blue 388' has become a veteran of many air displays the world over as it has partnered the similarly camouflaged Su-27UB 'Blue 389'. Here, the aircraft is being prepared for the afternoon's flying display at Farnborough '90. The trio of mirrors affixed to the canopy framing looks remarkably similar to the fitment present in the F-14 Tomcat (*Tony Holmes*)

Published in 1992 by
Osprey Publishing Limited
59 Grosvenor Street London W1X 9DA

© Osprey Publishing

ISBN 1 85532 152 1

Editor Tony Holmes
Page design by Paul Kime
Printed in Hong Kong

For a catalogue of all books published by Osprey Aerospace please write to:

The Marketing Department, Octopus Illustrated Books, 1st Floor, Michelin House, 81 Fulham Road, London SW3 6RB

A close study of this photograph, taken during a goodwill visit to Oklahoma City in June 1990, reveals virtually the whole spectrum of aviation, both modern, and not so modern. Besides the familiar shape of 'Blue 388' in the foreground, a Boeing 737-200, Cessna 172, Convair 340, several F-16s and an assortment of A-7D Corsair IIs can also be seen. The latter more potent types hail from the 465th Tactical Fighter Squadron (Air Force Reserve), and the 125th Tactical Fighter Squadron (Oklahoma Air Guard) respectively
(*Peter Wilson*)

Introduction

In Lockheed's own 'Air Power' magazine, YF-22 ATF (Advanced Tactical Fighter) project personnel referred to the Su-27 and MiG-29 with astonishing candour. One in particular made the following remarks: 'The Russians are hot fighter jocks and the Su-27 and MiG-29 are sportier than anything we have in the inventory . . . (but) the F-22 will have better manoeuvrability than the Su-27, which is top gun at the moment.' Clearly those involved in designing the USAF's next fighter believe that the Su-27 is superior to existing US warplanes, an opinion reinforced by impressive appearances by the Su-27 at Western air shows.

The remarkable airshow routines flown by pilots of both the Su-27 and the MiG-29 have demonstrated manoeuvres (such as the tailslide and the 'Cobra') which simply cannot be emulated by Western fighters. These have been dismissed by some as having no tactical relevance, since so much energy is lost, but this fundamentally misses the point. The tailslide, for example, demonstrates a remarkable degree of tolerance to intake disturbances on the part of the engines, and a remarkable degree of confidence in the aircraft's aerodynamic performance on the part of the pilot. Think about it. To safely fly such a manoeuvre at airshow altitude, it must be utterly predictable and repeatable.

In the West, the most agile fighters rely on sophisticated fly-by-wire control systems which bring with them hard edges to the flight envelope. The computer simply will not let the pilot overstress the aircraft, or risk departing from controlled flight.

Although agility is good, since natural stability is poor, high Alpha capability is modest. The Su-27 is also fitted with a fly-by-wire control system, but the flight envelope has soft edges—the pilot can override the various limiters, allowing him to achieve angles of attack in excess of 90°, beyond the area now being explored by dedicated research aircraft in the West.

This high Alpha capability, coupled with a helmet mounted sight and all-aspect missiles, makes the Su-27 an unrivalled close-in turn fighter, but it is important to realise that the air superiority, 'dogfighting' task is not the aircraft's primary mission. Instead, the Su-27 was designed as a long range interceptor, using sophisticated missiles to destroy targets at beyond visual ranges. To achieve this mission the Su-27 has a formidable range on internal fuel, and can carry six long range and four short range missiles, in addition to a powerful built-in 30 mm cannon.

Putting together the aircraft's long range and BVR capability with its undoubted capability as a dogfighting aircraft, the Su-27 can also function as an unbeatable escort fighter. Su-27s based in the Kola Peninsula could have escorted Tu-26 *Backfires* down into the UK Air Defence Region, while Polish based Su-27s could have reached Germany or even East Anglia. The USAF's F-15s would not find these big Soviet fighters easy opposition, and the RAF's unwieldy Tornado interceptors would have found them a real headache. It is just as well that the new era in East–West relations means that the *Flanker* is now unlikely ever to present a threat.

Right 'Blue 388's companion on its forays westward has been this awesome trainer, Sukhoi Su-27UB 'Blue 389'. Fully aerobatic, this aircraft has performed as many display routines as its single-place stablemate over the last three years

Contents

The Sukhoi T-10 – The first *Flanker*

The very first prototype Su-27 (then known only as the Sukhoi T-10) made its maiden flight on 20 May 1977, in the hands of Sukhoi's Chief Test Pilot, Vladimir Ilyushin. Soon afterwards, a Western spy satellite photographed the aircraft at Ramenskoye, leading to the allocation of the provisional reporting name *Ram-K*. This indistinct and fuzzy image remained the only picture of the new aircraft until 21 July 1985 when a Soviet TV documentary celebrating the life of Pavel Sukhoi (who had died ten years before) included a ten-second clip showing the first flight of the T-10. Not shown here are the prominent overwing fences which were removed from the prototype T-10 during the flight test programme. This particular aircraft, preserved at Monino since 1987, is believed to be the first T-10. This original configuration is known to NATO as *Flanker-A*. Clearly visible are the main undercarriage doors, which also acted as airbrakes, a la Folland Gnat (*Mark R Wagner*)

The Sukhoi T-10 prototype was a much lighter aircraft than the production Su-27, since it had no built-in cannon, much less internal fuel, and lighter engines. It was in an early configuration T-10 that test pilot Nikolai Sadovnikov had a narrow escape from death when, during a maximum speed test, the outer section of the port wing, and part of the port tailfin, broke off. The pilot brought the aircraft under control and landed safely. Sadovnikov is little known in the West, but was one of the pilots of the record breaking P-42, and flew a non-stop $15\frac{1}{2}$ hour endurance flight in the Su-27UB from Moscow to Komsomolsk-on-Amur and back. He has tested over 60 types, amassing 3500 flying hours and earning himself a Gold Star of the Hero of the Soviet Union, the Order of Lenin, and the Order of the Red Banner of Labour in the process (*Mark Wagner*)

Flanker forebear: the adoption of low-level penetration tactics by NATO left the Soviet Union's existing interceptors, typified by the Sukhoi Su-15 *Flagon*, virtually obsolete. Extensive modifications produced updated variants like the Su-21 *Flagon-F* seen here, but such aircraft were intended only as stop-gaps until a new generation of interceptors could be brought into service. This aircraft carries AA-3 *Anab* missiles outboard (SARH to starboard, IR-homing to port) and a pair of short range AA-8 *Aphids* inboard (*Via Paul Bennett*)

Sukhoi Su-21, AA-3 *Anab* missiles and underfuselage cannon pods—the combination which accounted for the ill-fated Korean Airlines Flight 007. The Boeing 747 was shot down on 1 September 1983 after overflying the Kamchatka Peninsula and Sakhalin Island. The incident showed the poor level of preparedness of the IA-PVO to deal with intruders, and demonstrated the reliance still being placed on tight ground controlled interception (GCI) by obsolete interceptors, whose short range meant that they had to strike quickly and return immediately to base. The Su-27, with its very long range and capacity for autonomous action, would have allowed the Soviet pilots more time to identify the intruder (*Via Paul Bennett*)

To fulfil its mission, the Su-27 combines a powerful weapons system with astonishing manoeuvrability and a breathtaking performance. The latter feature made it inevitable that Sukhoi would use the aircraft to try to break the time-to-height records set in 1975 by the McDonnell Douglas *Streak Eagle*. A similarly stripped and lightened aircraft, designated the P-42 (seen here), was used between October 1986 and March 1987 to set a series of 27 World time-to-height records, including several in the STOL (take off in less than 500 metres) category. For these records, the P-42 was flown by Victor Pugachev, Oleg Tsoi, Yevgeni Frolov and Nikolai Sadovnikov. On 29 March 1990, Pugachev used the P-42 to set a time-to-height record to 15,000 metres, carrying a 1000 kg payload, of 1 minute 21.7 seconds. Take off weight for the record attempt was 15,514 kg (7000 kg less than normal for a standard Su-27) while the R-32 engines each produced some 1100 kg more thrust than the standard AL-31Fs (giving a total of 27,200 kg). The P-42 features cropped tailfins, and has no ventral fins, armament or radar. The aircraft is unpainted

Zhuravlik in service

Raising the air force flag at a frontline base. A fully-armed alert *Flanker*, 'Red 29', sits at readiness outside its hardened aircraft shelter in the background. The aircraft carries AA-11 *Archer* IR homing missiles on the wingtips with AA-10 *Alamos* under the wings, under the engine nacelles and perhaps between the engines. The Su-27 is nicknamed *Zhuravlik* (or crane) in Soviet service (*Via Carey Schofield*)

Left The aircraft known to NATO simply as the *Flanker* also bears the design bureau designation T-10, and the air force designation Su-27. The T-10 type number indicates that the aircraft is the tenth Sukhoi design with a Delta (Treugolnyi or triangular) wing. Su-27 prototypes and development aircraft are sometimes referred to by longer designations, such as T-10-24 or T-1024, the latter indicating merely that the example aircraft was the 24th T-10 built. Here a production Su-27 taxies out for a training sortie (*Via Carey Schofield*)

Above The production Su-27 is a very purposeful (and different) looking machine. The prototype had suffered from severe aerodynamic problems, which necessitated a complete redesign. The twin fins had to be altered in size and shape and moved outboard to long booms beside the engine nacelles. The wing was extensively altered, losing its fences and receiving cropped tips, which incorporated combined flutter weight/missile launch rails. Leading-edge slats were added, and the nosewheel was repositioned further aft, and made to retract forwards instead of backwards. Finally, the main undercarriage doors were redesigned and an F-15 style airbrake was added to the spine. The redesign was a major task, and the first modified Su-27 (reportedly designated T-10-22 and thus probably the 22nd aircraft) did not fly until 20 April 1981. Here 'Red 04', a production Su-27, gets airborne in full 'burner (*Via Carey Schofield*)

Above Like many in-service Su-27s, 'Red 07' and 'Red 15' have all dielectric panels and radomes painted in dark green. This does little to enhance the air superiority blue grey camouflage, but does show the location of the flush HF aerial on the leading edge of the starboard tailfin (*Via Carey Schofield*)

Right The same two Su-27s in a loose echelon high above the motherland. Neither aircraft is armed, although both carry a full complement of pylons. The Su-27 serves mainly with the IA-PVO in defence of the Soviet Union, though a handful, including those based in Poland, serve with the air force as long range escort fighters (*Via Carey Schofield*)

Above 'I have control'. The instructor in the back seat lands this Su-27UB in text-book fashion, keeping the nose high to make maximum use of aerodynamic braking. Unlike most other two-seat versions of Soviet combat aircraft, the Su-27UB has no periscope for the instructor, whose view forward is surprisingly good (*Via Carey Schofield*)

Right An operational *Flanker* gets smartly airborne for a training mission, carrying a single AA-10 *Alamo* acquisition round (identifiable by the black stripes) under its port wing. This is a standard peacetime fit, since external fuel is never carried. Soviet runways, generally, are long and very wide, and parallel and linking taxyways give a huge number of potential take off strips on every airfield, even without the prepared grass strips and the ability of most Soviet combat aircraft to operate from semi-prepared strips. Typical Soviet hardened aircraft shelters are visible in the background (*Via Carey Schofield*)

Above 'Red 04' completes its landing run. The use of twin brake parachutes gives an enormous area and consequently high drag. A single chute of similar area would drag along the ground. A single AA-10 is visible beneath the port wing (*Via Carey Schofield*)

Right 'Red 04' lands back after a mission, slowed down by twin cruciform braking parachutes. The use of twin chutes is common in larger Soviet tactical aircraft like the Su-27 and MiG-25. The combination of white radome and green dielectric panels is quite common on service aircraft (*Via Carey Schofield*)

Above 'Red 61', an Su-27UB, taxies back after a training mission. The tip of the tailcone is open, showing that the aircraft has used its drag chute on landing. The aircraft in the background vary slightly, some having the unusual fin leading edge projections associated with early Su-27s, whilst others lack them (*Via Carey Schofield*)

Right Post flight a group of IA-PVO pilots compare notes before clambering aboard the GAZ jeep which will take them back to the mess for a refreshing bottle of Zhiguli, Russia's finest beer! Vladimir, cigarette in mouth, far left, obviously can't wait and has decided to skip the debrief and walk to the mess. With that kind of attitude he must be a staff officer or the unit commander, or perhaps the Political Commissar! (*Via Carey Schofield*)

At the close of the day's flying the aircraft are towed back to their shelters, cockpits already covered over. Life on an Su-27 squadron is far from idyllic, since normal operations are regularly hampered by shortages of even the most basic items of equipment. One Su-27 unit commander recently complained that his unit was short of 26 oxygen masks, 54 pilot's helmets, 24 throat mikes and an unknown number of flying boots (*Via Carey Schofield*)

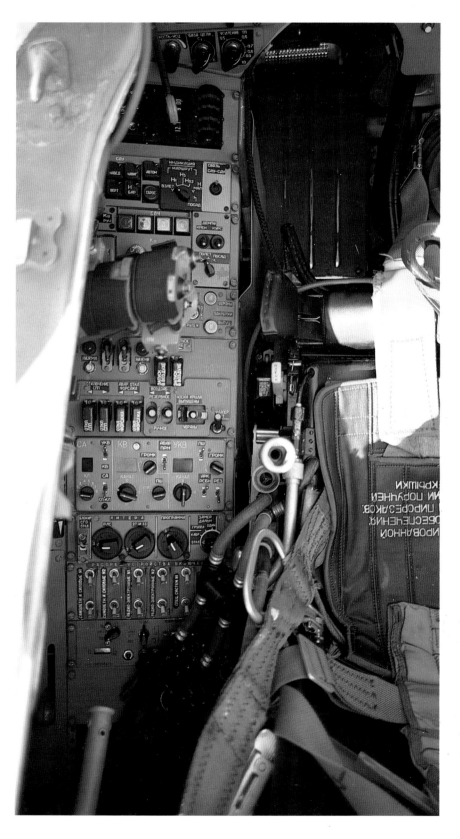

In the cockpit

Opposite The front cockpit of the Su-27UB demonstrator (the single seat cockpit is virtually identical). Yevgeni Frolov's aerobatic display routine, annotated in the 'Aresti' shorthand familiar to any Pitts pilot, is clipped to the glareshield. The *Flanker* cockpit is spacious and comfortable, and is broadly similar to the cockpit of the MiG-29 and other current frontline Soviet types, easing pilot conversion from other aircraft. The main panel has flight instruments at left, engine and systems gauges in the middle, and RWR, radar screen, warning panel and fuel contents at right

Left The left hand console incorporates fuel system switches, start-up panel, communications, radio compass and oxygen system controls. The twin throttles are mounted on 'slide rods' on the side of the cockpit wall, and are similar to those found in the MiG-29

Above The right hand console accommodates various weapons system switches, environmental system controls, and a warning panel. The overall feel of the Su-27 cockpit is that it is better laid out than that of the contemporary MiG-29, and broadly equivalent to the cockpits of Western aircraft like the F-15. Sukhoi claim to have flown a modern glass cockpit in the Su-27

Right The pilot's Head Up Display is identical to that of the MiG-29, and incorporates small sensors for tracking the pilot's Helmet-mounted sighting system. This gives the pilot an invaluable off-axis target designation capability, and allows him to launch a missile without using radar, or 'boresighting' his target

Opposite The left hand side of the main panel contains six main instruments. Clockwise from top left are the combined α/g meter, the ASI, the attitude indicator, the Horizontal Situation Indicator, the barometric altimeter, and the radar altimeter. Below these six main dials are the undercarriage, control surface and flap position indicator, and the clock

Left The rather chunky stick-top of the *Flanker* incorporates various switches and selectors. Weapons systems triggers are on the rear face (one is shown cocked and ready for use) with braking controls further down on the stick. At far left is what is described as 'the manual control for using radar missiles in the optical mode'. Next to that, the red button serves as an autopilot disengage button and also activates the datalink. In the centre is a pitch and roll trimmer while at far right the white painted button is a re-orientation button, which will return the aircraft to straight and level flight from any attitude. Mounted below this array of buttons is a sliding Long/Short Range selector

Below The simple radar warning receiver (RWR) display of the Su-27 is seldom photographed. Lights show whether the threat radar is in the forward or rear hemisphere, and separate lights show the approximate bearing; 10°, 30°, 50° or 90°. A row of lights across the bottom of the instrument can be programmed to light up to indicate various different types of threat radar

An overview of the Su-27 cockpit. The K-36D ejection seat has no 'remove before flight' pins, and is armed by simply snapping the ejection handles into an upright position, then made safe by pushing them back forward. Padded leg restraints line the inner walls of the foot wells, and in the event of ejection these are pulled in towards the outer edges of the seat by thick cables, bringing the pilot's legs with them and preventing flail injuries. Small arm restraints are also fitted to the sides of the seat

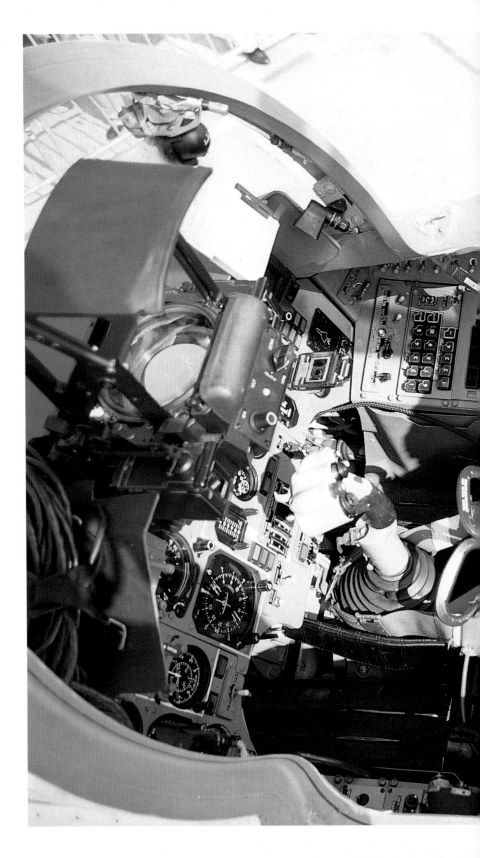

Walk round

Right The Su-27 *Flanker* incorporates a sophisticated Infra Red Search and Track System (IRST), with a collimated laser rangefinder. This allows the Su-27 pilot to detect, track and even engage a target without making radar emissions, which might warn the enemy pilot of his impending demise. While the IRST is operating, the radar is switched on and is slaved to follow the target, but is not transmitting. If IRST contact is lost (perhaps because the target flies into cloud) the radar automatically begins transmitting. The mirror-like reflector focuses IR energy into the dark area in the centre and is articulated to move in elevation, while the whole unit inside the glass 'ball' moves in azimuth

Below A close-up view of the IRST 'ball' showing the motors which drive the 'collecting mirror' in elevation (*Joe Cupido*)

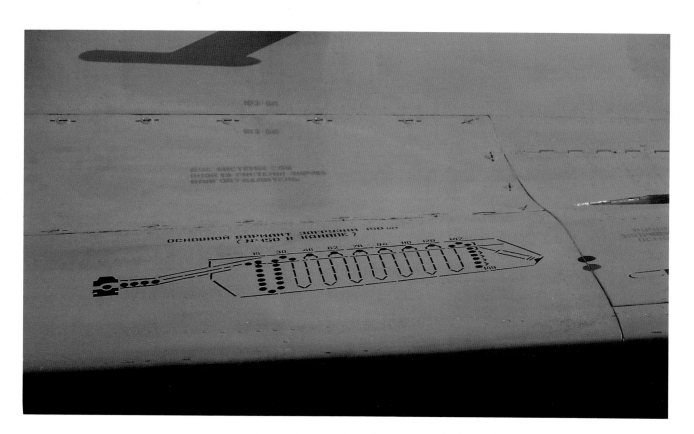

Above This stencil on the port LEX (leading edge extension) shows the location and layout of the ammunition tank, and the way in which ammunition is fed across the fuselage to the gun in the starboard LEX. The cumulative totals of ammunition in each section of the tank is included, with the first fifteen rounds housed in the feed to the gun itself

Above left The graceful radome of the Su-27 is believed by many to accommodate the same NO-193 *Slot Back* multi-mode pulse Doppler radar as is used by the MiG-29. This would seem unlikely, since the radome diameter is much larger, and since *Flanker* reportedly lacks the multiple target-engagement capability claimed for the MiG-29. It is possible, however, that the *Flanker*'s fire control radar may be a more powerful derivative of an early version of the MiG-29's NO-193, with a larger antenna. Small vortex generators are mounted at the base of the pitot probe

Left Although it is optimized for BVR (Beyond Visual Range) interception, the Su-27 does incorporate a built-in 30 mm GSh-301 cannon, with 149 rounds of ammunition. The cannon is housed in the starboard wing leading edge root extension, and the muzzle projects out behind a huge titanium blast shield. On the two-seater (shown here) this blast shield is even larger, extending upwards almost to the cockpit sill. A series of small vents behind the gun prevent the build up of dangerous gases when the weapon is fired

Above Located just aft of a rectangular dielectric panel on the nose is a prominent Angle of Attack vane, a critical piece of equipment in an aircraft with such a superb high α performance. Further aft still is a small white sphere. This is a forward hemisphere antenna for the radar warning receiver system

Left The cockpit canopy of the Su-27 gives the pilot an excellent all-round view, comparable with that enjoyed by the pilots of modern Western fighters. The centreline location of the IRST blocks the view forward over the nose slightly, and there is a heavy frame behind the pilot's head, but these would make little difference during air combat. Access to the cockpit is via a purpose-built ladder. Also visible in this view are three of the five piltot probes dedicated to gathering air data for the fly-by-wire control system

Above Frequently used access panels, like this one for the INS and other mission avionics systems, remain attached to the aircraft even when removed

Right The nose gear of the Su-27 houses three landing/taxy lights and is equipped with its own powerful pneumatic brakes. Soviet designers mistrust hydraulic systems, which rely on inflammable liquid, and prefer to use pneumatics (which rely on air) wherever possible. A pneumatic reservoir is attached to the inner face of the nose gear door

Above The nosewheel of the Su-27 incorporates a heavy-duty mudguard which prevents loose gravel, mud, snow or stones being thrown up during rough field operations. The mudguard fitted to the Su-27UB (shown here) differs in detail, incorporating slots in the rear to allow foreign objects to be ejected downwards, and to reduce drag on take-off

Right The engine intakes of the Su-27 incorporate meshed FOD protection screens. These are automatically actuated (by pneumatics) when the engines are started, and hinge downwards to lie flat in the base of the intake after rotation on take-off. They deploy again on landing (*Joe Cupido*)

The engine intakes are sharply raked, giving excellent characteristics throughout a wide angle of attack range. They incorporate a plethora of variable ramps, bleed slots and spills to control mass flow and give maximum control of shock wave formation in the intake itself. As with all supersonic intakes, shock waves are deliberately generated to slow down and pressurize incoming air before it reaches the compressor face. A prominent radar warning receiver antenna is mounted on the side of the intake, adjacent to the lower lip

The main gear of the Su-27 is simple and strong, with a single oleo. The mainwheels retract forwards, swivelling through 90° to lie flat horizontally. Unusually, a small bracing strut linked to the oleo locks into a fairing on the engine nacelle after undercarriage extension. The wheels themselves are each equipped with an integral cooling fan, allowing very heavy braking

Right The two Sukhoi demonstrator aircraft wear the Bureau's stylized logo on their tailfins. This incorporates the cyrillic letters 'SU' in a dart shape, superimposed on a circle. In-service *Flankers* and many other Sukhoi types frequently wear a more representational 'wing' badge, often wrongly identified as a unit marking

Opposite A stencil marking on the rear fuselage and ventral fin shows the limits of tailplane travel, from 16° up to 21° down

Below Ventral fins were added to the production Su-27 to enhance directional stability, especially at high angles of attack. The tailfins themselves were increased in size and were moved outboard at the same time. Similar ventral fins originally fitted to the MiG-29 were later omitted to save weight, Mikoyan having discovered that the aircraft's directional stability at high α was already adequate

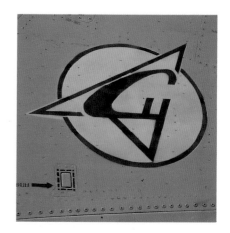

Above A long bullet fairing projects aft from between the engine nozzles of the Su-27. Capped by two dielectric fairings which serve the RWR system, the fairing can also accommodate a seldom-used brake parachute, and a variety of chaff and flare launchers

Right The long tunnel between the engine nacelles can carry a pair of missile pylons in tandem. When fitted, these usually carry a pair of short-burn Semi-Active Radar Homing (SARH) AA-10A air-to-air missiles. One navalised *Flanker* was seen with what appeared to be a small camera pod fitted in this position

Above The business end of the Su-27's 27,650 lb st Lyulka AL-31F augmented turbofan. The afterburner nozzles incorporate inner and outer jet pipes, like those of the MiG-29. The twin-spool AL-31F has a four-stage fan, a nine-stage high pressure compressor, a single stage high pressure turbine and a two-stage low pressure turbine. The afterburner has multiple radial spray bars and two flameholders. The engine has a remarkably high TBO (time between overhaul) of 1000 hours, and a life of 3000 hours, although every 100 hours they are checked by borescope, oil analysis, and vibration monitoring equipment (*Joe Cupido*)

Right The afterburner of the AL-31F. The radial fuel sprays and the flameholders are visible. Afterburner (or reheat, call it what you will) takes the AL-31F's maximum thrust from 17,857 lbs st in military power to a staggering 27,560 lbs st. Fuel consumption rises even more rapidly!

Above Pugachev straps into his Severin K-36D zero-zero ejection seat. The same basic model is used in the MiG-29, and was convincingly demonstrated at Paris in 1989 when Anatoly Kvotchur had to bail out of his MiG-29 when he lost control after an engine failure during a low speed, low altitude flypast. Prominent fairings beside the headrest contain stabilising telescopic drogue arms

Left With his walk-around complete, Victor Pugachev straps on his helmet. The modern Soviet flying helmet is light and comfortable, and is cut well away from the face, giving an excellent field of view. An inflatable bladder inside the helmet can be used to clamp the helmet very firmly to the head, and this is activated automatically in the event of a cockpit depressurisation or on ejection. Pugachev favours a throat microphone for displays, disdaining an oxygen mask and built-in microphone

Paris debutante

Left Like many Soviet aircraft before and since, the Sukhoi Su-27 made its public debut in the West at Le Bourget during the 1989 Paris Air Salon, alongside the giant six-engined Antonov An-225, the Il-96-300 'Airbus', the Tupolev Tu-204 '757ski' and the combat-proven Sukhoi Su-25 *Frogfoot*. The *Flanker* stole the show, flown by Victor Pugachev in single seat form, and by fresh-faced Yevgeni Frolov in its two-seat incarnation. Even in the static display, the Su-27 proved a magnet for the Parisian crowds

Below One of the many who successfully negotiated themselves a static park pass and gained access to the Su-27 for a sketchy briefing on the aircraft and its cockpit. One very senior *Armée de l'Air* officer took one upmanship a step further by arranging a familiarization flight for himself!

Above Late each morning the Sukhois were towed from the static park to a hardstanding beside the taxyway, where they were fuelled and made ready for their flying display. Here the single seater still has its tow bar attached

Right Late in being towed to the hardstanding one day, Pugachev dons his helmet while the groundcrew struggle to remove the towbar. Pugachev did not miss his display slot, though he did cut it very fine

Left The crowdline, and the balconies of the various hospitality chalets, were always densely packed for the Sukhoi display. Head on, the drooped nose of the *Flanker* is immediately obvious

Above Pugachev's Su-27 gleams in the sun as he waits for take-off clearance to begin his display. The code '388' was applied as a Paris show code, and was retained on this aircraft for its subsequent trips to Singapore, the USA and Farnborough

Above The Sukhoi's nose oleo compresses as the engines are run up to full military power against the brakes. The brakes are then released, the aircraft begins to roll forward, the 'burners are engaged and '388' hurtles down the runway to begin its display

Right Climbing steeply into the blue to begin his first public display in the West, Pugachev probably didn't even notice the British Airways Lockheed TriStar trundling sedately towards *Aeroport de Paris Charles de Gaulle*. With both engines in full reheat the Su-27 climbs like an arrow, especially when lightly loaded for an airshow demonstration. The spectacular take offs had the crowds gasping

Above The Su-27 flies by for a high α pass in the hazy summer sunshine. One manoeuvre silenced every critic, a dynamic deceleration in which the aircraft briefly pitched back to an angle in excess of 90 α before returning to straight and level flight. They dubbed it 'Pugachev's Cobra', and it had a similar impact to the MiG-29's much-discussed tailslide at Farnborough the year before

Above right The *Flanker-B* stabilized on finals, dorsal airbrake, leading edge slats and trailing edge flaps deployed. The Sukhoi Su-27's similarities to the McDonnell Douglas F-15 Eagle are readily apparent in this view

Right '388' over the piano keys at Paris, seconds from touchdown. The very high angle of attack on finals is particularly noteworthy. This is adopted to reduce the landing speed as much as possible, albeit with the slightly greater risk of 'grounding' the engine nozzles. During the Paris Salon Frolov in the two-seater did scrape his tailpipe on the runway, but no damage was caused

Left The cockpit was always occupied while the *Flanker* was under tow, but the canopy was left open to keep it cool. Progress from the static park to the taxyway was slow, due to the huge crowds, all of whom seemed to want to get as close as possible to the Su-27

Above As the Su-27UB is towed into position for refuelling, the significantly smaller two seat MiG-29UB taxies past to start its display. The crash of the single seat MiG-29 early in the show did not ground the MiG-29s at Paris, and Mikoyan pilot Roman Taskaev did his best not to allow the bigger Sukhoi to steal the limelight

Members of the groundcrew prepare the Su-27UB for a display flight, checking the various systems quickly but efficiently. When not busy moving or looking after the two *Flankers* the brown-suited engineers seemed to be on a perpetual hunt for badges, ballpoint pens and other souvenirs, for which they were happy to swap Sukhoi tie pins. As the week went on, they became progressively more businesslike, striking harder and harder bargains in their quest for nick-nacks

Above Frolov waits patiently for taxy clearance, leaving the canopy open for as long as possible. The Sukhois at Paris had a good surface finish, and their groundcrews clearly took pride in their charges

Left Frolov conducts a last minute conference at the foot of the boarding ladder, familiarizing himself with the latest details of the serviceability of the aircraft and its systems, and discussing any problems with the technicians. By Western standards the Su-27 is maintenance intensive, and that a four-man groundcrew is necessary even for a normal turnaround. In the air force, where some would be conscripts, and where aircraft would need to be re-armed, even larger numbers would be needed

Above 'Bit early on the landing, Hoskins'. Frolov, clearly a devotee of 'Flight's' Uncle Roger Bacon, lands in the undershoot. The two-seat Su-27UB flew a virtually identical display to that flown by the single seater, although many observers rated Frolov as the better display pilot. Unlike the MiG-29UB, which has no radar, the Su-27UB retains full operational capability, although internal fuel capacity is slightly reduced

Right Frolov frequently dragged the Su-27UB in on a long, fast, flat approach, but this is considered more normal in Warsaw Pact air arms. The two-seater was very new in 1989, and it was only a few weeks before Paris that the first photos of an Su-27UB were released. At this time, frontline Su-27 regiments relied largely on MiG-23UB *Floggers* for training

Above Frolov taxies in after a display, watched by his waiting groundcrew. He has already cracked the canopy open for improved ventilation. The aircraft will now be defuelled and returned to the static aircraft park. The Su-27s did not return to Paris for the following Salon in 1991, due mainly to economic pressures

Right Fresh-faced Yevgeni Frolov, a highly experienced aerobatic pilot on the Su-26, is also one of the main Su-27 demonstration pilots. He was also one of the test pilots involved in the record breaking P-42 flights

Sukhoi over Singapore

Well-known aviation photographers Chris Allan (familiar to regular Osprey customers with his 'Fast Jets' and 'Dogfight' volumes) and Katsuhiko Tokunaga found themselves with a scoop when Sukhoi asked them for assistance in arranging an air-to-air photo trip. The two snappers found the RAAF keen to conduct a joint sortie with two of their F/A-18s, so Tokunaga took the back seat of one of the Hornets, while Allan's camera ship was a Pilatus PC-9 demonstrator flown by test pilot Hans Butschi. The photo-flight led to further contacts, culminating in a demonstration flight for Air Marshall Ray Funnell, RAAF Chief-of-Air-Staff (*Katsuhiko Tokunaga*)

Wing Commander Ross Fox, OC No 75 Squadron, flies a neat echelon on the single seat Su-27, flown by Victor Pugachev. The mixed formation flew a series of manoeuvres, and it quickly became apparent to the Australian pilots that the larger Sukhois could accelerate and decelerate very quickly indeed, and they frequently had to engage 'burner to keep up. Tragically, Wing Commander Fox was killed in a mid-air collision with another F/A-18 from RAAF base Tindal, Northern Territory, in August 1990 (*Katsuhiko Tokunaga*)

Above The two-seat *Flanker* rolling. The Su-27UB was flown by Yevgeni Frolov, with Aeroflot navigator Victor Gorbatov in the back seat translating for the Sukhoi test pilots and handling the radio. The two-seat F/A-18 was flown by Flying Officer John Corbett, a young line pilot from Tindal-based No 75 Squadron (*Chris Allan*)

Right RAAF Chief of Air Staff Ray Funnell with Pugachev before his historic flight. Although this was severely curtailed by the fading light and the obstruction displayed by Changi air traffic control, Air Marshall Funnell did put the Su-27 through its paces flying some high *g* turns, a loop and a series of slow and aileron rolls. 'It handled all those with considerable aplomb and exhibited excellent handling characteristics', was his later verdict (*Chris Allan*)

Pugachev demonstrates his Cobra. Airspeed decays from 200 to about 65 knots, with a height loss measured in tens of feet. Manoeuvres like the tailslide and 'Cobra' do have a limited tactical significance. The tailslide is an excellent last-ditch method of spoiling an opponent's firing solution, or of turning the tables in a vertical scissors, while the 'Cobra' demonstrates an ability to point the nose (and gun, missile seeker heads, etc) a long way 'off axis', and is a phenomenal way of decelerating very quickly. The lost energy can be quickly regained by using the enormous levels of thrust and low aerodynamic drag (*Sequence by Katsuhiko Tokunaga*)

A beautiful study of the single-seat Su-27 *Flanker-B* in flight. The aircraft's humped back and drooping nose, together with its angular lines, give it a purposeful but unmistakably Soviet air. The *Flankers* shown at Western airshows have never carried even dummy missiles, and lack many items of military equipment. The effectiveness of the *Flanker*'s unique three-tone blue-grey camouflage at medium level can easily be gauged, as can the reason for white, instead of dark green, radome and dielectric panels

Flanker in the USA

Left Gorby's flying circus comes to town. The first visit by the Sukhoi Su-27s to the USA was made during 1990, and the two aircraft flew to Oklahoma City to participate in the air show there. On their way into the USA, the two Sukhois were escorted into US airspace by the F-15s of the 21st Tactical Fighter Wing based at Elmendorf AFB, Alaska, and from the alert detachments at Galena and King Salmon. The two Su-27s were dwarfed by their support ship, the mighty Antonov An-225 Mriya (Dream) when they arrived at Oklahoma City, escorted by a pair of Grumman F-14 Tomcats (*Air Photo via Joe Cupido*)

Below The big Antonov wheels around to join the circuit while Yevgeni Frolov taxies in in the Su-27UB. Later in the week, an American female aerobatic pilot was reportedly given a flight in the Su-27UB, becoming the fourth Western pilot to sample the *Flanker*, following French, Singaporean and Australian senior air force officers who were flown at Paris and at Asian Aerospace (*Joe Cupido*)

Below The Sukhoi's presence at Oklahoma City shattered many illusions. Beside an aircraft that was demonstrably the World's biggest transport, were two sleek, modern looking fighters which could fly a better airshow demonstration routine than any US aeroplane. Confidence that the USA built the World's best fighter planes may not have been smashed in one visit, but doubts about the size of America's lead were certainly planted in many minds *(Peter Wilson)*

Right The prominent dorsal airbrake of the production Su-27 is clearly visible in this view of the single-seat *Flanker* landing after an energetic display routine by Pugachev. Landings are usually made without a drag chute, using aerodynamic and heavy wheel-braking instead *(Joe Cupido)*

Above These two Sukhoi Su-27s were pictured, at Boeing Field during July 1990. Due to attend Seattle's 'Goodwill Games' their participation in a flypast with two US Navy Intruders was marred by the refusal of the US pilots to continue with the planned display after one of the Su-27s barrel-rolled round them over the Cascades! Interestingly, these aircraft are not the pair used by the Sukhoi OKB for sales and demonstration work, and were reportedly assigned to the Soviet Space Agency and used in the same way that NASA uses its T-38s (*Peter West*)

Right The two Su-27s flying trail on a Sukhoi Su-26MX over Oklahoma. Planned participation by the *Flankers* at a number of other US airshows was cancelled after the Sukhoi crashed, and the two fighters returned home. This was not the last chance to see Su-27s in US skies, however, since two different aircraft, flown by different pilots, visited twice more during 1990 (*Katsuhiko Tokunaga*)

Above 'Red 14' was at Payne Field in Washington State from 10 to 21 August 1990. The two Space agency aircraft returned to participate in Payne Field's airshow as a thank you for Payne's help during other Su-27 visits to the USA. This aircraft was written off on 9 September 1990 when it failed to recover from a loop during an airshow at Salgareda/Treviso in Italy. The pilot, Rimas Stankiavicius, had recently been appointed chief test pilot for the Soviet shuttle programme and was killed in the crash (*Arnold Swanberg*)

Above left The winged badge seen on the tailfins of 'Red 05' and 'Red 14' has been described as an older version of the Sukhoi OKB badge, and has often been seen on in-service Sukhoi aircraft, from the Su-17 to the Su-24, -25, and -27. The dark green dielectric panels and radome of 'Red 14' have been seen on many in-service Su-27s, while the two-letter codes are typical of IA-PVO Regimental codes (*Peter West*)

Left The sheer size of the Su-27 cannot be gauged from this photo of 'Red 05' being escorted by a Montana ANG 'Viper'. Despite its size, the Soviet fighter is no less agile, and can accomplish manoeuvres no F-16 pilot would dare emulate. Moreover, when all the kit is working, the Sukhoi has genuine BVR capability and a passive detection, tracking and engagement system in the shape of its IRST. There can be few F-16 pilots who wouldn't like to sample the big Sukhoi (*Montana ANG*)

Farnborough *Flankers*

The same two *Flankers* that had thrilled the crowds at Paris, in Singapore, and in North America made the type's British debut at the Farnborough air show in September 1990. The two aircraft arrived in a tight formation after their flight from Moscow. Some said they had staged through an operational *Flanker* base in Western Poland, others that they'd flown non-stop. The two Sukhois made a neat pairs landing, touching down on the numbers, watched by a small gaggle of photographers and pressmen. Although the MiG-29s had claimed the honour of being the first Soviet fighters in Britain two years before, there was still plenty of interest in the bigger Sukhois, and many enthusiasts thronged the minor roads outside the airfield, waiting for a first glimpse of these rare visitors. After touchdown Pugachev cracked open his dorsal airbrake slightly to keep station with the draggier two-seater. The latter two-seater was flown by Yevgeni Frolov, with an Aeroflot navigator in the back seat. Ground support equipment and groundcrew were carried over in the huge An-225 *Mriya*, also making its British debut

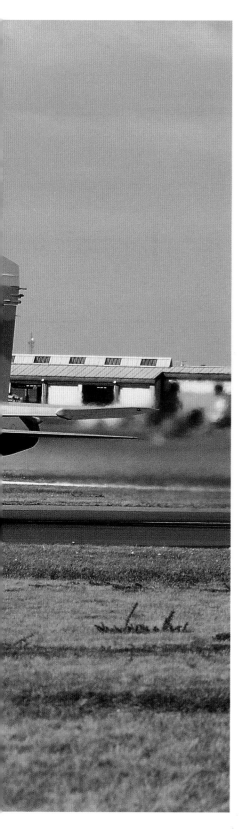

Above On 7 September, there was a rare evening flight by the Su-27UB. On board, strapped into the front seat, was Britain's Chief of the Air Staff, Air Chief Marshal Sir Peter Harding. Sukhoi have tended to give front seat rides to prestige figures (often senior officers) whereas Mikoyan have concentrated on giving (usually back seat) familiarization flights to active, current jet pilots or defence analysts. In order to conserve fuel, to allow Harding to gain maximum benefit from his flight, the Su-27UB took off without afterburner. Another familiarization flight was given at Farnborough on 4 September, this time to David North, managing editor of 'Aviation Week and Space Technology', who thus became the·only Westerner to have flown in both the Sukhoi Su-27 and the MiG-29

Left The single-seat Su-27 begins its take-off roll, its humped back giving the aircraft the air of a crouched panther, ready to spring. Pugachev's displays at Farnborough were extremely memorable, including his famous 'Cobra' and an impeccable tailslide. The Mikoyan team included a Cobra in their routine, too, showing the friendly rivalry which exists between the two Design Bureaux

Connected up ready for towing, the Su-27UB is soon to be moved from the static park to the north side, to be prepared for its afternoon flying display. The same cockpit access ladders can be attached to the rear fuselage to give access to the tail unit and top surfaces (*Tony Holmes*)

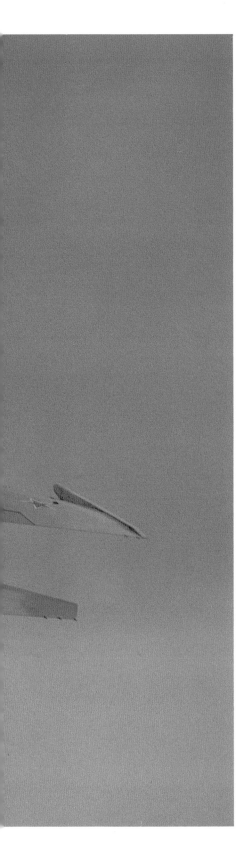

Above Shock wave 'diamonds' are clearly visible in the afterburner plume of the Su-27UB as it accelerates down the runway with Frolov at the controls. The reason for the inner surfaces of the undercarriage doors being painted red is uncertain

Left The Su-27UB gets smartly airborne, the two big Lyulka AL-31Fs pushing out a staggering 55,000 lbs of thrust-equivalent to more than one and a half Tornados or Hornets! Afterburning thrust exceeds normal take-off weight by more than 3000 kg, and the aircraft at Farnborough were operating with minimum fuel and no weapons! (*Tony Holmes*)

Above The gear is retracted quickly after take-off to avoid exceeding the limiting speed for the undercarriage and doors. The nosewheel retracts forwards, while the mainwheels each rotate through 90° before folding forwards to lie flat in the underside of the wing root

Left With 'burners blazing, and with a shimmering heat haze behind it, the Su-27 leaps into the air. The normal fuel load for displays was less than half the maximum capacity of 19,000 lbs, and allowed generous margins for delays and diversions even after the afterburner–heavy display routine. The operational radius of the *Flanker* is extremely impressive, even without external fuel or inflight refuelling. These latter options are available on the naval variant of the Su-27

Above In virtual silhouette, from the rear, the Su-27 looks more like a refugee from Star Wars than a modern fighter. Only a full authority digital fly-by-wire control system could keep such an unstable shape flying, although Soviet FBW actually allows the pilot to deliberately go beyond what would be 'hard limits' on a Western equivalent

Left The Su-27 shows off its undersides during a display. Clearly visible are the auxiliary air inlets on the undersides of the main intake ducts, and the way in which the air intakes 'toe in' towards each other. The Su-27 features some very advanced aerodynamics, which give it its phenomenal high α performance, and which keep air flowing into the intakes

Above After touchdown, it is usual to keep the nose up, letting the huge wing act as an efficient airbrake, generating huge amounts of drag. Although a brake parachute can be fitted in the tailcone, this has seldom been used during Western visits

Left Farnborough 1990 (it could hardly be anywhere else) and the Su-27UB is on finals, twin landing lights ablaze, after an energetic display

Above Farnborough farewell. The two Su-27s depart from Farnborough after a successful fortnight of displays, demonstrations and bridge-building. The two-seater led the pair away from Farnborough. Flown by Yevgeni Frolov, an English-speaking Aeroflot navigator occupied the back seat, manning the radio. Eager to save fuel, the two aircraft took off in military power, but were still airborne after a relatively short run

Above left The nosewheel has its own independent braking system, and when this is used, the aircraft slows down very rapidly indeed, compressing the nosewheel oleo quite dramatically, and flinging the pilot forward in his straps (*Tony Holmes*)

Left Dorsal airbrake fully deployed, the Su-27 coasts down the runway before turning right on to the parallel taxy track. Dorsal airbrakes give little trim change when used, and are thus very popular. The trend-setting F-15 featured this airbrake configuration, and so will Europe's next generation fighter, the EFA (*Tony Holmes*)

Frontal *Flankers*

Left One of the first Westerners to see an active frontline *Flanker* was German photographer Martin Baumann, who captured five Su-27s on film as they returned to their base at Chojna in Poland. Chojna has usually been described as an Su-24 *Fencer* bomber base, but has in fact long had at least a fighter element. In February 1990, for example, the *Fulcrum*-C made its first deployment outside the USSR to Chojna, and today the Su-24s in Poland are based at Szprotawa, Osla and Zagan. Chojna's Su-27s seem to wear black nose codes with blue tail codes. 'Black 61' is an Su-27UB, one of only three Su-27UBs based at Chojna, and one of six in the whole of Poland (*Martin Baumann*)

Below Usually thought of as being a PVO interceptor pure and simple, the Su-27 is also used in substantial numbers by the Strategic Air Armies of the air force, and even by Frontal Aviation, as long-range escort fighters. It is said that by operating from Poland, *Flankers* could escort Su-24s or Tu-26s to targets in eastern Great Britain. More Su-27s may be transferred to air force command, since the IA-PVO disgraced itself during the abortive coup against Mikhail Gorbachev in August 1991, and may face disbandment. The PVO Chief of Staff blocked the use of Gorbachev's aircraft while the leader was under house arrest and the C-in-C urged support for the 'Emergency Committee' which ousted Gorbachev. Their attitudes contrasted sharply with those of their air force equivalents who resigned from the Communist party alongside Boris Yeltsin and refused to participate in operations against the defenders of the Russian Parliament (*Martin Baumann*)

Left 'Black 24' is obviously the pride of its crew chief, having won the pentagonal shield and 'paper dart' shaped 'excellence' award. The significance of the seven small red stars above this is unknown, as is the two-tone finish on the radome. The grey and blue camouflage looks particularly 'weathered', perhaps indicating that this aircraft is one of the older *Flankers* still in service (*Martin Baumann*)

Above Su-27s are also based at Kluczewo (sometimes incorrectly known as Stargard) in Poland. 'Red 48' and 'Red 51' from the Kluczewo-based 159th Fighter Interceptor Regiment visited a number of Eastern European airshows during late 1991, including Poznan-Krzesiny in Poland and Kbely in Czechoslovakia. For their airshow appearances the two Su-27s (36911027307 and 36911027310) were flown by Captains Alexander Dudarenko and Alexander Michaljov, 'ordinary' air force pilots who quickly showed that Farnborough and Paris-style displays were not only for highly experienced OKB Test pilots (*Hans Nijhuis*)

Bitburg-based F-15C Eagles in the background lend scale to the enormous *Flanker*, whose gigantic proportions make its agility even more astounding. At the airshow in Poland, Bitburg F-15 drivers were among the first to explore the cockpits of the big Sukhois (*Hans Nijhuis*)

Russian Knights

Left The first overseas visit by the *Russian Knights* (preceded by a visit to Rheims in France by the Proskurovsky Guards' MiG-29-equipped *Swifts* second squadron) was made to Britain. Nominally staged to allow the team to participate in the 'Battle of Britain' Displays at Finningley and Leuchars (actually their public debut, having only practised in private in the USSR), the visit also marked a response to the Red Arrows visit to the Soviet Union in 1990. Appropriately enough, the Russians were based at and hosted by RAF Scampton, home of the Central Flying School, parent unit of the Red Arrows. The team brought six *Flankers*, including two Su-27UBs, one of which led the four aircraft display formation. For those interested in such things, the two-seat aircraft were coded '18' (1040804) and '19' (1040807). The single seaters were '04' (36911031412), '05' (36911031513), '07' (36911031615) and '10' (36911031614)

Below The *Russian Knights* hail from a base at Kubinka, near Moscow, which actually houses an entire divsion with three full Regiments, each with three squadrons. Long associated with demonstration and aerobatic flying, the first squadron of the Kubinka-based Proskurovsky Guards Regiment consists of the *Russian Knights* display team, whose aircraft wear a patriotic red, white and blue colour scheme, with tailfins bearing the air force blue and yellow 'sunburst' flag

Left The badge of the Proskurovsky Guards Regiment is worn on the starboard intake (and on right hand flying suit shoulders!). The legend at the top literally says 'KUBINKA' in cyrillic script, and the one on the bottom says 'PROSKUROVSKII'. The date 1938 refers to the year in which the Regiment was formed, although the name and the Guards status were picked up during what Russians still call the 'Great Patriotic War' of 1941 to 1945

Below Ten pilots of the Proskurovsky Guards Regiment, including the five men who actually form the *Russian Knights* display team, and various Regimental 'Wheels', all of whom are first class or Sniper pilots. Most if not all of these highly experienced fighter pilots were flown in RAF Hawks or Tornados during their brief stay, while some RAF pilots were flown in the two-seat Su-27UBs

Below 49-year-old Lieutenant-General Nikolai Antoshkin, Commander of the Moscow Military District's air forces, leads from the front, and flew one of the Su-27UBs into RAF Scampton. Antoshkin represents the new generation of Soviet air force senior officers – a professioal aviator determined to display the not inconsiderable achievements and skills of those he commands

Above A head-on view of one of the single-seat *Flankers*. The prominent wing leading edge root extensions which give *Flanker* its superb high α performance are shown to advantage, as are the box-like wedge air intakes. Tiny vortex generators can just be seen at the base of the pitot probe

Above left The hump-backed Sukhois taxy through the murk on arrival at Scampton, passing one of the ground instructional Hawker Hunters, a classic fighter from a much earlier generation. The aircraft taxied in slowly, with steam and smoke seeming to seep from a multitude of orifices

Left The *Russian Knights* wore an unusual colour scheme, which was basically applied on top of standard camouflage. The nose was painted white, and red, white and blue bands encircled the upper fuselage, with the red and white bands extending down the leading edges of the wing, and repeating themselves on the tailplanes. Behind these stripes, the aircraft wore standard camouflage on their top surfaces

Above Unfortunately, the one press facility arranged for the visit of the *Russian Knights* did not include access to the edge of the runway, so the various photographers could only watch in frustration as the team performed a neat finger four take-off

Right The *Russian Knights* display consists of manoeuvres by a four-ship formation, interspersed by one (and sometimes two) solo aircraft. Holding rock steady formation, the team's display included an incredible low speed high α flypast, as well as looping and rolling manoeuvres. Formation changes, however, were conspicuous by their absence. A slightly ragged practice at Scampton on arrival day (18 September) gave way to polished performances at the 'Battle of Britain' show at Leuchars and Finningley on 21 September, and reportedly at the special Balmoral flypast staged specifically for the Queen Mother, honorary Air Commodore and Commandant in Chief of the Central Flying School, and who General Antoshkin had hoped to meet

The six Su-27s arrived at Scampton in thick grey cloud and intermittent drizzle, escorted by four Tornado F.3s from No 29 Sqn. The Tornado is by no means a small fighter, but was dwarfed by the enormous *Flanker*. A mass flypast was made before the Tornados went back to Coningsby, including a low-level turn which left the innermost Tornado pilot dropping out of formation to avoid scraping his wingtip along the grass. 'Should have tucked in tighter', mused one *Flanker* pilot afterwards *(Ian Black)*

Above The second two-seater, '19', was used by Colonel Basov to lead the four aircraft formation, and for some of the familiarization flights. Rails for an instrument flying training hood are visible in the front cockpit. Unlike the two-seat MiG-29UB, which has no radar, the Su-27UB retains full operational capability

Above left As with the Sukhoi demonstration pilots that have thrilled crowds the world over, the *Russian Knights* recovered from their polished display with a perimeter fence scraping runway approach

Left The first RAF officer to be flown by the *Russian Knights* was Air Marshal Sir John Thomson, Air Officer Commanding RAF Support Command. As far as can be determined, it seems that the Russians did not fly a single current RAF air defence fighter weapons or tactics instructor in the Su-27, with the RAF nominating various senior officers, a Tri-national Tornado Training Establishment squadron commander and three of the Red Arrows instead. A missed opportunity, or a realistic view that nothing of great significance would be learned in short demonstration flights?

Few could have dared predict that one day six Su-27 *Flankers* would be sitting on the apron at RAF Scampton. The Su-27's huge entry ladder incorporates provision for a small brush, allowing a pilot to quickly remove any mud or snow from his boots before entering the cockpit. The red, white and blue colour scheme of the team's aircraft is based on the colours of the Russian flag and was applied during August and September 1991. By Air Forces Day on 18 August only two aircraft had been painted up. The team had not displayed before an audience until they visited England, although a single solo aircraft (in full markings) did appear at the Air Forces Day display at Tushino. The team apparently has a pool of pilots from which to draw, including at least two young captains, but the pilots who flew in the UK were all majors or higher. 'We're very impressed by their professionalism' confided a Red Arrows pilot, 'and we don't say that lightly'. Relations between the two teams were cemented in a series of social events, including sampling Webster's Yorkshire Bitter in the 'Arrows crew room and a visit to the pub, a novelty specifically requested by the Russian pilots who were eager to imbibe large quantities of . . . what they saw as the traditional English way-of-life!